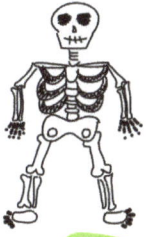

My name is _____

and I am going to the hospital! The hospital I am staying at is called _____

_____(name of hospital) and it is

located in _____ (city, state).

I arrived at the hospital on _____ (date)

and I am being treated for _____

_____

Hospital Address (for Thank You Notes):_____

🌸 Emergency Contact Information 🌸

Name:_____   Relationship:_____

Phone:_____

Name:_____   Relationship:_____

Phone:_____

PREPARE AHEAD Hospital Checklist

Cross out each item after it is packed/prepared

1. Change of clothing, pajamas, socks, slippers, bathrobe
2. Electronics - tablet, phone, computer
3. Extension cord, charging cords for electronics
4. Download new apps to pass the time, games, learning
5. Second favorite toy and blankie (what if it gets dirty?!)
6. Pillow, pillowcase
7. Books to read, school work
8. Gifts or treats for your hospital staff and caregivers
9. Personal toiletries:

    hand soap, body soap, toothpaste, toothbrush, lotion
10. Face/baby wipes
11. Favorite snacks/drinks in a small cooler, water bottle
12. Anything that provides comfort

    (recommend things that are washable)
13. Glasses, contacts
14. Bath/shower toys
15. Colored pencils, crayons, markers, THIS BOOK!
16. Bluetooth speaker for calming music
17. Current medications and medical history on next page
18. (your item here)_____

MEDICATIONS & MEDICAL HISTORY

Medications + Dosage:

_____

_____

_____

_____

_____

_____

_____

Medical History:

_____

_____

_____

_____

_____

_____

_____

PCP _____ Phone _____

Prepare ahead of time and tape pictures on these 4 pages so you have your friends and family with you during your hospital stay!

tape pictures here!

Instagram @Hospital_Kids

tape
pics
here!

photos

↓

MY QUESTIONS FOR THE DOCTOR OR NURSE

_____

_____

_____

_____

_____

_____

_____

_____

_____

_____

_____

_____

_____

_____

MY QUESTIONS FOR THE DOCTOR OR NURSE

Ask your friends and family to sign their name in your book on these 4 pages

VISTORS

VISTORS

VISTORS

SEEK AND FIND

Look for the following items in the hospital and in your hospital room.
Cross them off after you find them!

Heartrate monitor

Pulse oximeter

IV fluids in a bag

Blood pressure cuff

Hospital bed

TV

Remote control

Chair

Pillow

Syringe

Oxygen

Emergency Room

Computer

Gloves

Antibacterial gel

Janitor

Instagram @Hospital_Kids

SEEK AND FIND

Look for the following items in the hospital and in your hospital room
Cross them off after you find them!

Doctor

Hospital Library

Information Desk

Tree or plant

Nurse

MRI or CT scan machine

Medical Records Folder/File

Stethoscope

Band Aid

Gauze

X-Ray

Wheelchair

Face mask

Crutches

Ambulance

Cafeteria/Cafe

INTERVIEW

Circle one: Doctor   Nurse   Nurse Practitioner   Physician's Assistant   Janitor   Other Staff

NAME:

How long have you worked at this hospital?	Where did you study medicine?
What city are you from?	What year did you graduate?

What is your favorite part about this job?

How did you know you wanted to do this job?	What is your favorite thing to do in this city?

INTERVIEW

Circle one: Doctor   Nurse   Nurse Practitioner   Physician's Assistant   Janitor   Other Staff

NAME:

How long have you worked at this hospital?

Where did you study medicine?

What city are you from?

What year did you graduate?

What is your favorite part about this job?

How did you know you wanted to do this job?

What is your favorite thing to do in this city?

INTERVIEW

Circle one: Doctor   Nurse   Nurse Practitioner   Physician's Assistant   Janitor   Other Staff

NAME:

How long have you worked at this hospital?

Where did you study medicine?

What city are you from?

What year did you graduate?

What is your favorite part about this job?

How did you know you wanted to do this job?

What is your favorite thing to do in this city?

Instagram @Hospital_Kids

INTERVIEW

Circle one: Doctor   Nurse   Nurse Practitioner   Physician's Assistant   Janitor   Other Staff

NAME:

Make up your own questions!

WRITE A SHORT STORY

_____

_____

_____

_____

_____

_____

_____

_____

Draw a picture with it:

WRITE A SHORT STORY

Fill in the missing letter

Scr_bs

H_sp_tal

He_rt

 B_nes

Do_t_r

Nur_e

Emerg_n_y

X-R_y

Stethosc_pe

Do you have a window in your room? If so, what do you see?
What is the weather like?

_____

_____

_____

_____

_____

What is your favorite sport or activity?   My best friend's name is:

_____   _____

draw a picture

I go to school at _____

and I am in the _____ grade.

My teacher's name is _____

Draw a picture of yourself as a superhero!

Start

End

Instagram @Hospital_Kids

List of 20 things that make me HAPPY:

1. _____
2. _____
3. _____
4. _____
5. _____
6. _____
7. _____
8. _____
9. _____
10. _____
11. _____
12. _____
13. _____
14. _____
15. _____
16. _____
17. _____
18. _____
19. _____
20. _____

Write down your name and the names of your family members.
Then use the letters to create new words!

The first thing I will do when I get out of the hospital is _____

Draw a bouquet of flowers to brighten your day!

word search

```
T T R A E H Y E
F O E C F E P S
G C M F L A N A
R H E Y U L E E
E O R P I T G S
T S G P D H Y I
U P E A S G X D
P I N H U R O Y
M T C B L O O D
O A Y S E N O B
C L F E S R U N
W D O C T O R X
```

Blood
Bones
Computer
Disease
Doctor
Emergency
Fluids
Happy
Health
Heart
Hospital
Nurse
Oxygen

HOW MANY WORDS CAN YOU FIND?

circle the words!

Words hidden in the hearts:
PROUD, KIND, TOO, SAFE, SPECIAL, LOVED, PLAY, FUNNY, FAMILY, LAUGH, SMILE, CARING, HAPPY, HEALTHY, DOCTOR, NURSE, BODY, MIND, HEALING, HOSPITAL, GOOD, ATTITUDE, HEART

learn about the
body with the
SUPER SCIENCE
SERIES
by April Chloe
Terrazas

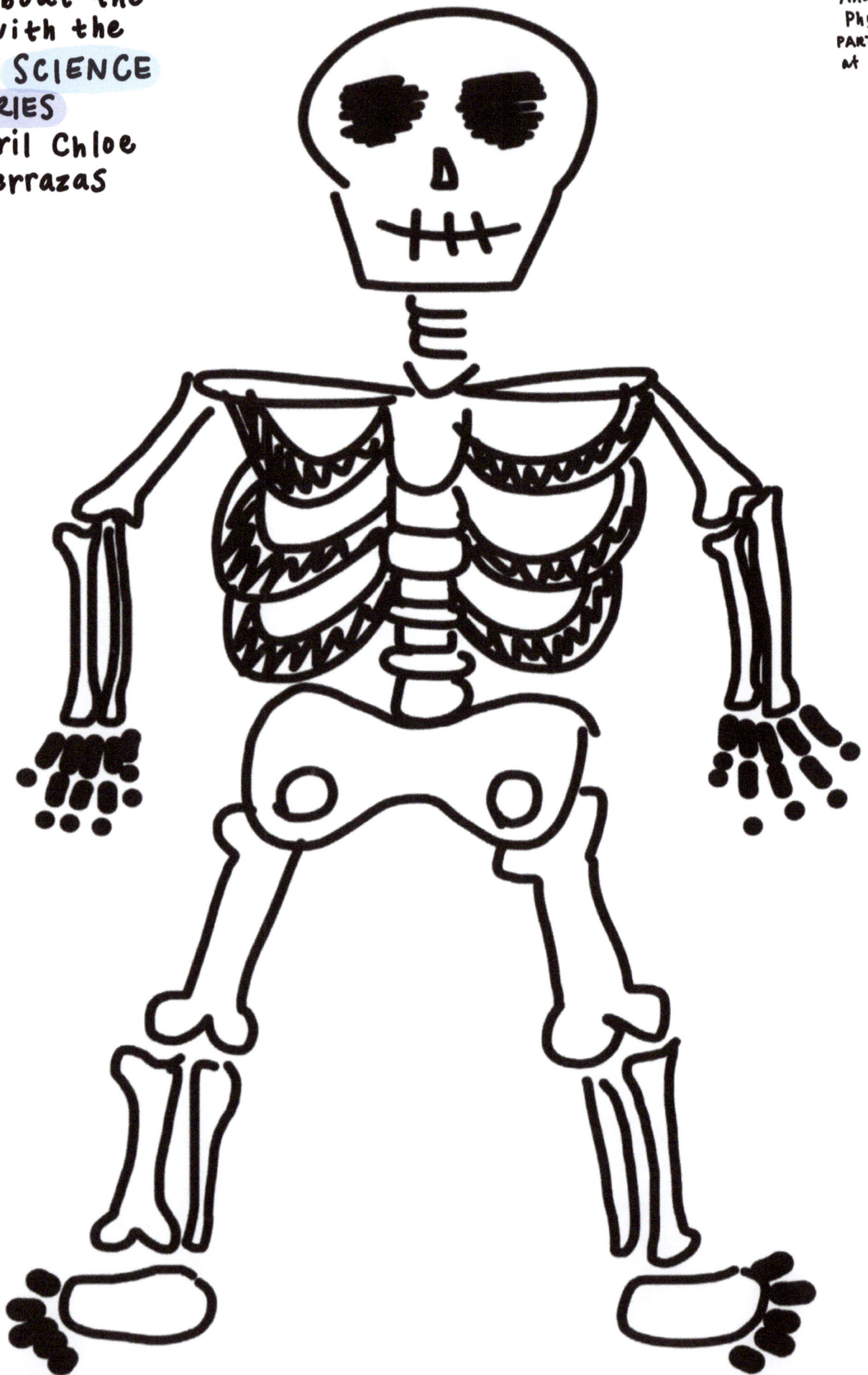

The 5 FUNNIEST words I can think of are:

1
_____

2
_____

3
_____

4
_____

5
_____

The nicest person I know is:

When I grow up, I want to

I am happiest when

```
Q  J  R  Y  Z  R
N  U  R  S  E  O
H  E  A  R  T  T
F  A  T  D  E  C
E  N  O  B  E  O
F  B  L  O  O  D
```

Blood
Bone
Doctor
Nurse
Heart

If you could describe yourself with ONLY ONE WORD, it would be

Start

End!

Draw a picture of a happy dog

What would you say to the sick or injured person in the next room to encourage them and lift their spirits?

_____

_____

_____

_____

_____

Instagram @Hospital_Kids

WHAT IS IT LIKE...

...to get a CT scan?

_____

_____

...to get blood drawn?

_____

_____

...to have surgery?

_____

_____

...to get a shot?

_____

_____

...to get an MRI?

_____

_____

What did you experience while in the hospital?

_____

_____

WHAT IS IT LIKE...

A B C D E F G H I J K L M N O P Q R S T U V W X Y Z
Z Y X W V U T S R Q P O N M L K J I H G F E D C B A

use this backwards alphabet code to write secret notes!

WORD Scramble

HPOSILTA _____

CTDORO _____

HELAHTY _____

HREAT _____

NBOE _____

ISCK _____

HPPAY _____

Fill in each word with the correct color

Red Pink Orange Green t ☆

B ☆ white

Black yellow rain

blue

Pur Light bow

ple green black

Red white Pink

green black

blue orange

Word Scramble Answers
Hospital, Doctor, Healthy, Heart, Bone, Sick, Happy

What is your favorite joke?

What is something that <u>always</u> makes you laugh?

BONES!

Epiphysis

Periosteum

Nerves

Blood Vessels

Diaphysis

Epiphysis

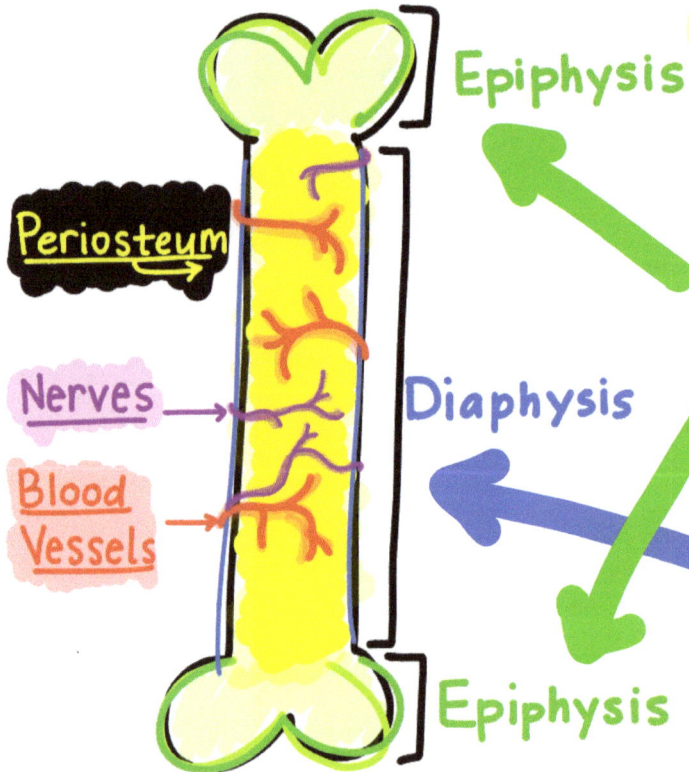

PER-EE-OS-TEE-UM
a membrane covering the outer surface of bones and has nerves and blood vessels.

E-PIF-EH-SUS
The end of a long bone.

DI-AF-EH-SUS
The shaft of a long bone.

OS-TEE-ON
Layers of dense bone with a canal inside for blood vessels.

SPUN-JEE BONE
Porous bone containing bone marrow and surrounded by compact bone.

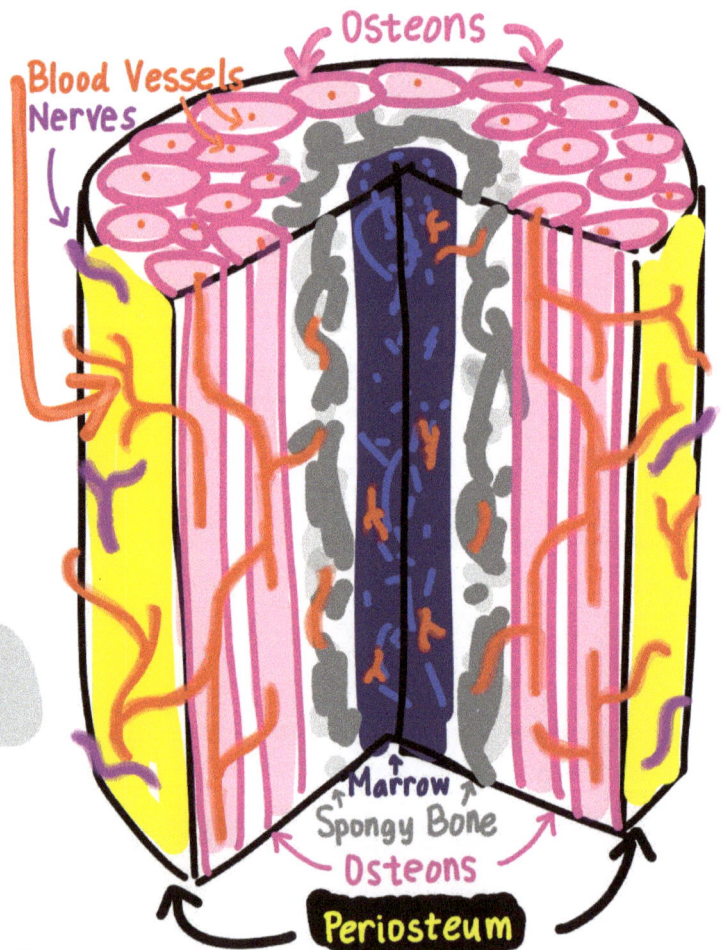

Blood Vessels
Nerves

Osteons

Marrow
Spongy Bone
Osteons
Periosteum

MER-O

Bone marrow is in the inner (middle) part of the bone. Marrow is a soft fatty substance that makes red blood cells.

KOM-PAKT BONE

The outer layer of bone made of osteons and periosteum.

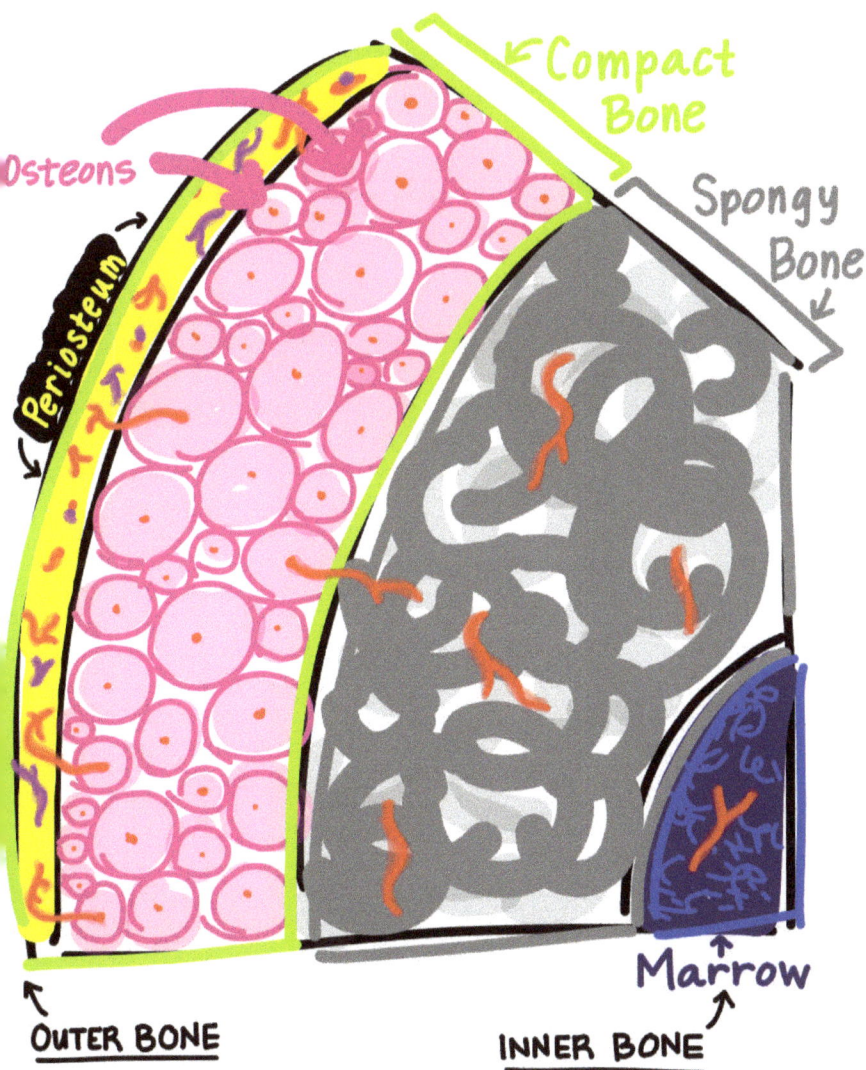

Osteons

Periosteum

← Compact Bone

Spongy Bone

Marrow

OUTER BONE

INNER BONE

POINT TO THE...

blood vessels

nerves

marrow

compact bone

spongy bone

periosteum

osteons

Complete the diagram

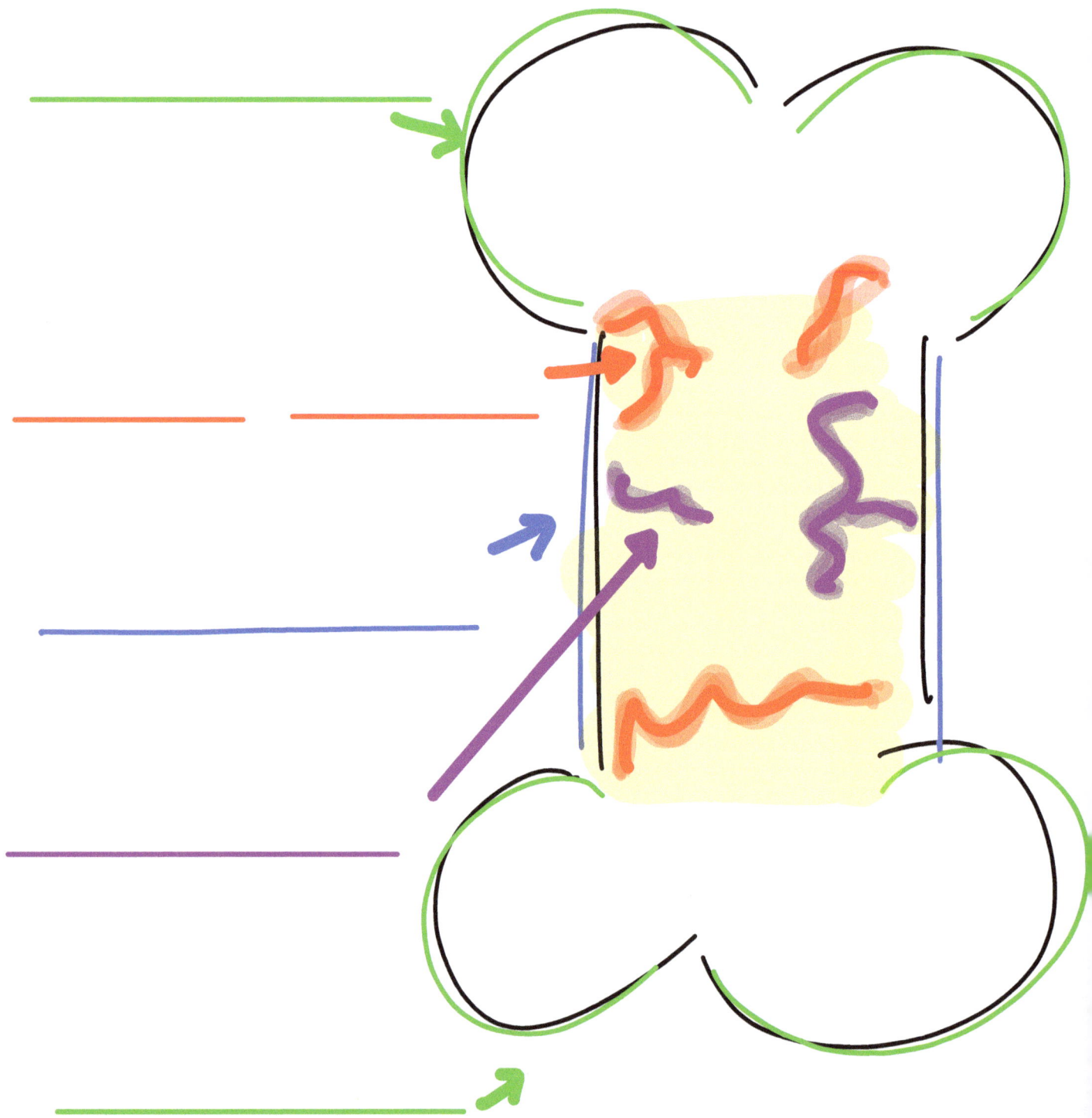

☐ Explain each part of the bone to an adult!

Complete the diagram ☺

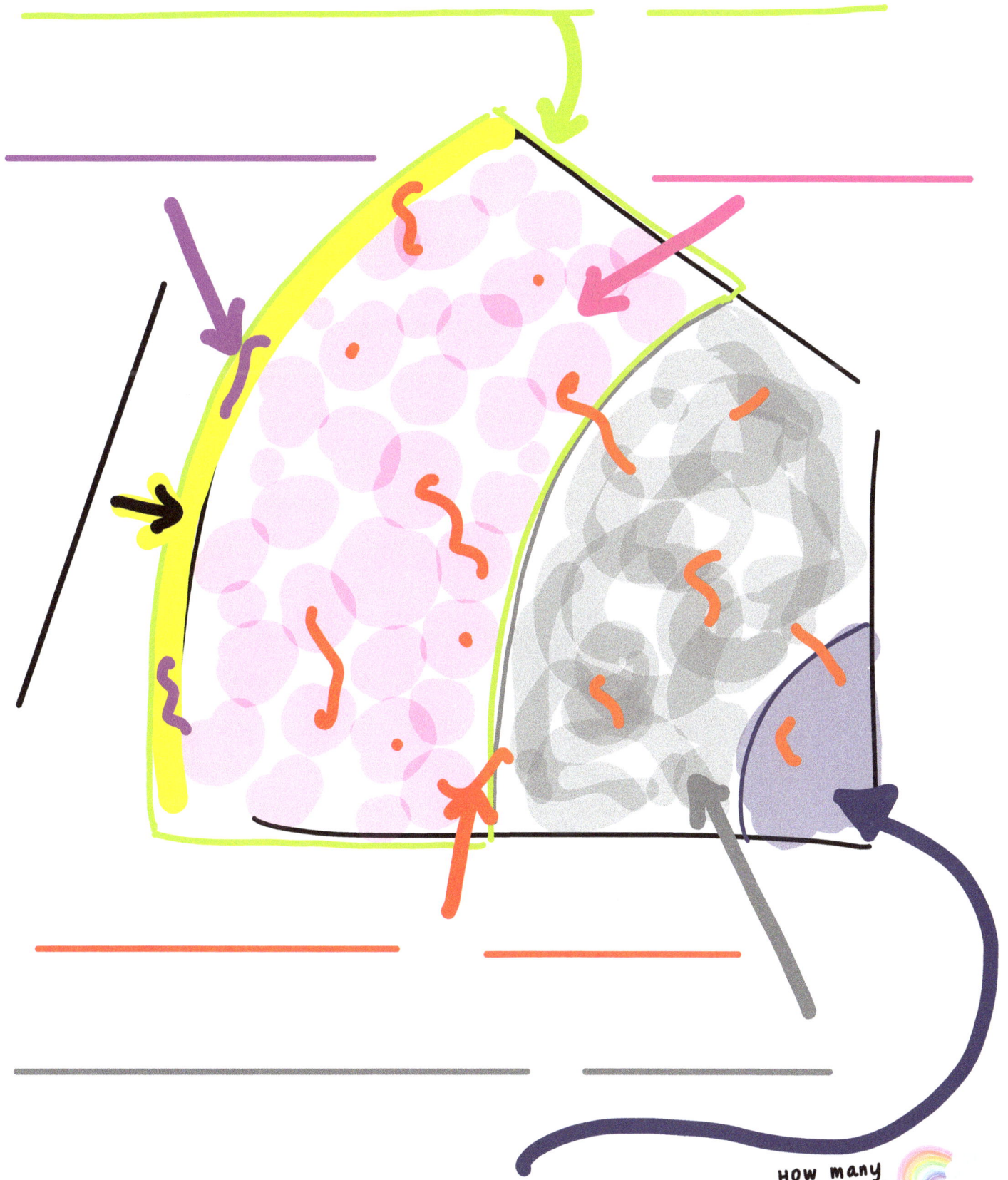

How many rainbows are in this book?↗

TIC TAC TOE!

Instagram @Hospital_Kids

DRAWING PAGE!!!

Thank You!

Fill in these Thank You Notes for your caregivers, cut them out and put it in an envelope.

Mail it to them using the address you wrote on page 1.

*

Use the remaining pages to design your own cards and fill in a note on the back!

*

Design your own cards using page 51.

write your own Thank You note on pages 48, 50 and 52.

Thank You!

Thanks!

Dear Dr. _____,

Thank you for helping me get better! You were so kind and patient with me and I appreciate it very much! ☺

Love,

_____

Thank You!

Thank You!

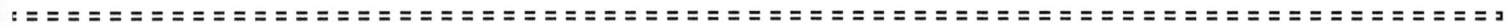

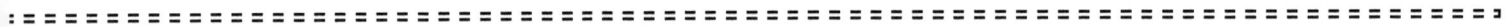